WORLD'S
TOUGHEST
PUZZLES

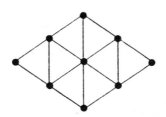

Charles Barry Townsend

 Sterling Publishing Co., Inc.   New York

This book is dedicated to our dear friend Laura, who loves life and lives every moment of it with sparkle and grace.

Edited by Timothy Nolan

Townsend, Charles Barry.
  World's toughest puzzles / by Charles Barry Townsend.
      p.   cm.
    1. Puzzles.   I. Title.
  GV1493.T688   1990
  793.73—dc20   89-49131
                                                        CIP

10   9   8   7   6   5   4   3

First paperback edition published in 1991 by
Sterling Publishing Company, Inc.
387 Park Avenue South, New York, N.Y. 10016
© 1990 by Charles Barry Townsend
Distributed in Canada by Sterling Publishing
% Canadian Manda Group, P.O. Box 920, Station U
Toronto, Ontario, Canada M8Z 5P9
Distributed in Great Britain and Europe by Cassell PLC
Villiers House, 41/47 Strand, London WC2N 5JE, England
Distributed in Australia by Capricorn Ltd.
P.O. Box 665, Lane Cove, NSW 2066
Manufactured in the United States of America
All rights reserved

Sterling ISBN 0-8069-6962-8   Trade
               0-8069-6963-6   Paper

Contents

Introduction

Welcome one and all to another session of mental stim-
ulation. This is the third book in our series covering what
we consider to be the world's greatest puzzles. As before
we've combined excellence with variety. In the following
pages you will encounter problems dealing with penguins, coins, paper, numbers, juggling, archaeology, bell
ringers, stockings, bottle caps, and sea horses. As with
the two previous collections, all these puzzles have stood
the test of time. The problems presented here may be five
years old or 105 years old but all are designed to test your
skills and please your puzzling palates. So, put away your
cares for a few hours and try your hand at solving over 70
of the *World's Toughest Puzzles.*

PUZZLES

The World's Toughest "Surveyor" Puzzle

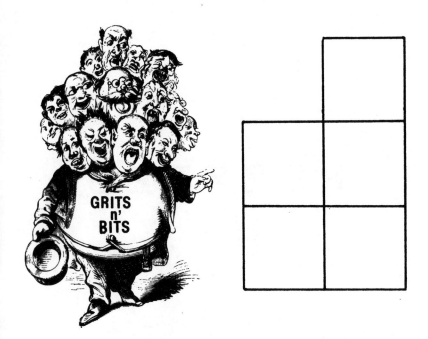

A surveyor stopped by the Grits-N-Bits coffee shop the other day and told about a job he had just finished. Two farmers had bought five square acres of land that had divided their farms and had asked him to lay out a straight fence that would divide their purchase into two equal parcels of land. After much thought, the surveyor came up with the answer. The only trouble is that he left town before telling anyone how he did it. Can you tell the folks at the Grits-N-Bits how it was done?

The World's Toughest "Mental" Puzzle

The digit that the young lady crossed out was a four. Is that correct?

Of course it's correct! The Mental Wizard never fails! Here's how to do it. Have someone blindfold you; then have them write down a large five digit number. Multiply it by 9, and instruct the person to cross out any digit they want to in the result. Finally, tell them to add up the remaining digits and to tell you what their sum is. With this information you can immediately tell them the digit that was crossed out. It's amazing!

The World's Toughest "Poem" Puzzle

Ten weary footsore travellers
　All in a woeful plight,
Sought shelter in a wayside inn
　One dark and stormy night.

"Nine beds—no more," the landlord said
　"Have I to offer you;
To each of eight a single room,
　But the ninth must serve for two."

A din arose. The troubled host
　Could only scratch his head;
For of those tired men no two
　Could occupy one bed.

The puzzled host was soon at ease—
　He was a clever man—
And so to please his guests devised
　This most ingenious plan

A B C D E F G H I

In room marked **A** two men were placed;
　The third he lodged in **B**
The fourth to **C** was then assigned;
　The fifth retired to **D**.

In **E** the sixth he tucked away
　And in **F** the seventh man;
The eighth and ninth in **G** and **H**
　And then to **A** he ran.

Wherein the host, as I have said,
　Had laid two travellers by,
Then taking one—the tenth and last—
　He lodged him safe in **I**.

Nine single rooms—a room for each—
　Were made to serve for ten,
And this it is that puzzles me,
　And many wiser men.

The World's Toughest "Penguin" Puzzle

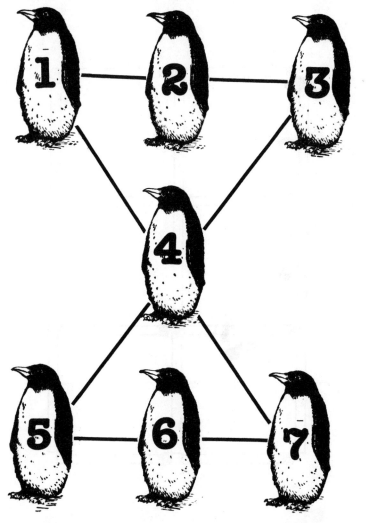

The puzzling penguins have waddled out to present our next problem. As so often happens with penguins they have forgotten their places. Can you reposition them so that their numbers add up to 12 horizontally, vertically and diagonally?

The World's Toughest "Match" Puzzle

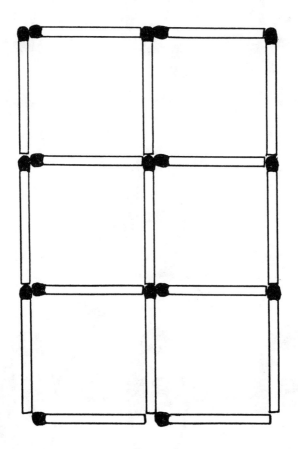

In this striking puzzle you must prove that six minus six equals two. In our matchless illustration there are six squares formed using 17 matches. Remove six of these matches so that only two squares remain. It's your move!

The World's Toughest "Coin" Puzzle

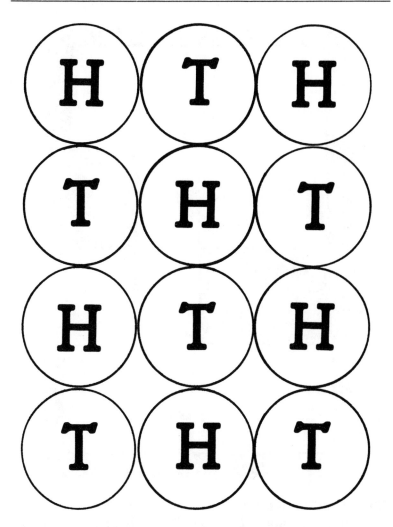

Lay out 12 coins on the table as shown here with six heads and six tails showing. Note that each of the four rows of coins contains a mix of both heads and tails. Now, by touching only one of these coins make the four horizontal rows either all heads or all tails.

The World's Toughest "Paper" Puzzle

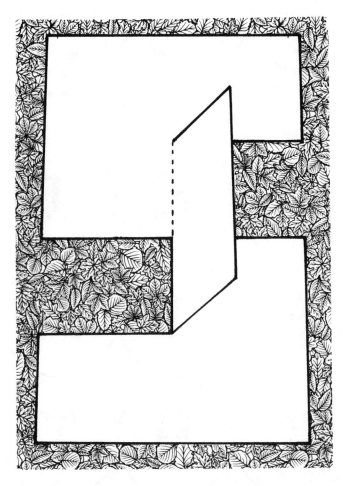

The above "impossible" paper puzzle is made using just one sheet of paper. The "flap," which moves back and forth, is part of the sheet, and it has not been cut out and glued back down. The area of the flap is exactly the same as the area of the two cut out sections of the paper. Yet the illustration is plainly an impossibility. So how was this paper puzzle created?

The World's Toughest "Portrait" Puzzle

The young artist pictured here won a commission to paint the portrait of this year's grand puzzle contest winner. Little did she know that the subject would be the puzzle itself. Undaunted, she not only executed the portrait in grand style but also solved the puzzle while painting it. After loading up her brush with plenty of paint she drew the picture shown here using one continuous line. At no time did she remove the brush from the canvas nor did she allow the line to crossover itself at any point. Can you render a similar solution?

The World's Toughest "Change" Puzzle

Please, Mr. Wellheeled, could you go over that puzzle once again before the trolley arrives? Rodger does so like a good problem!

Of course, Mrs. Crustworthy, it goes like this: Mr. Smith holds his closed fist out to Mr. Jones and says, "In this hand I am holding two coins. The sum of these coins comes to exactly 55 cents. One of the coins is not a nickel. Can you tell me the value of each of the coins?" I'll wager 55 cents that Rodger can't solve that one in less than five minutes!

Can you beat out Rodger and claim an award from Mr. Wellheeled?

The World's Toughest "Progression" Puzzle

The winner of the giant $1,000 puzzle contest is Mrs. Winifred Spellright

12, 1, 1, 1, 2, 1, 3, _, _, _, _

It seems that the other contestants in our annual puzzle contest are not taking the good fortune of Winifred Spellright very well. The puzzle was to figure out what the next four numbers should be in the progression puzzle pictured above. Get your handkerchiefs ready, you only have five minutes to solve this one.

The World's Toughest "Archaeology" Puzzle

'WHAT WALKS ON FOUR LEGS IN THE MORNING, TWO LEGS IN THE AFTERNOON AND THREE LEGS IN THE EVENING'?

Those intrepid archaeologists, Hawkings and Petrie, have dug up another relic from the past. Let's listen in:

"At last, Petrie, we've discovered that sensational monument from the past, the famous 'Riddle of The Sphinx.' It must be all of 3500 years old!"

"What do you mean, *we*," sputtered Petrie, "leave me out of this! I hardly think that the puzzlers of the Pyramids wrote in English!"

The monument is a fake, of course, but the riddle is a good one. See if you can solve it while Hawkings and Petrie check the lads downstream.

The World's Toughest "Bell Ringer's" Puzzle

Brother Sebastian and Brother Thaddeus are on clock tower duty. From the look of things I'd say that they're in for a hectic night. Normally when the bell is in working order they are fairly consistent in their work. For example, it takes them exactly 25 seconds to ring out 5 o'clock. Given these facts, can you tell how long it takes them to ring out 10 o'clock?

The World's Toughest "Talisman" Puzzle

Pictured here is the talisman of that famous gambler J. Wellington Moneybags. Unfortunately the printer put the numbers in the wrong places, causing the charm to lose its power. To restore its strength you must rearrange the numbers one through nine so that the total of four numbers along any one side will be 17. The numbers at the corners will, of course, be included in the totals of the adjacent sides.

The World's Toughest "Checker" Puzzle

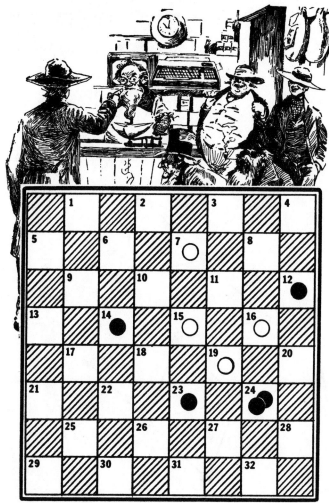

Pop Bentley, down at the general store, can still play a mean game of checkers. Above is the end of a game he won from Cy Corncrib the other day. Pop was playing the white pieces and it was his turn. Can you figure out what moves won the game for him? The white pieces are moving up the board while the black are moving down.

The World's Toughest "Triangle" Puzzle

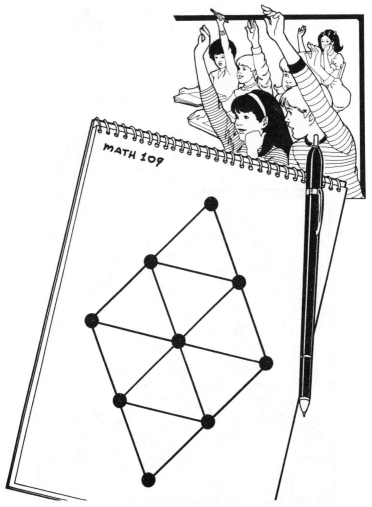

The kids seem to know the answer to last night's math stumper. The geometric figure in our notes has eight triangles formed with 16 bars. The problem is to remove four of the bars so that you are left with just four equal-sized triangles. You have five minutes to complete this assignment.

The World's Toughest "Stocking" Puzzle

SIR·ROJER·DE·ROMILY·ROSE
HAD·AT·LEAST·SIXTY-FIVE—
SUITS·OF·CLOTHES
HIS·CRAVATS·OF·ALL·STYLES
MEASURED·MILES·UPON·MILES
WHILE·HIS·RUFFLES·
AND·FRILLS

GOODNESS KNOWS!

Although Sir Rojer played the part of a fop he is reputed to have been an excellent swordsman. Early one morning, while dressing for one of the many duels that he fought during his checkered career, he went looking for a pair of matching stockings. In the bottom drawer of his dresser he knew that he had ten pair of white stockings and ten pair of grey stockings. However, the light from the single candle atop his dresser was too dim for him to discern white from grey. Can you determine what the least number of single stockings would have to be removed from the drawer so that he would be sure of having one pair of matching stockings to put on when he got outside in the light?

The World's Toughest "Measuring" Puzzle

Many years ago, so the tale goes, two good old boys, Billy Bones and Pester Pew, got in an argument down at the Bucket O'Blood grog shop. It seems that Billy came in with an empty five-gallon cask and asked Pester to put four gallons of his finest rotgut rum in it. Unfortunately the only measure in the house was an old three-gallon pewter jug. Try as they might Pester and Billy just couldn't figure out a way to measure out exactly four gallons from the rum vat using these two receptacles and as you can see, their frustration soon evolved into mayhem. If you had been there, could you have solved their problem?

The World's Toughest "Alice" Puzzle

Alice, on her way to the Mad Hatter's Tea Party, came to a fork in the path that she was following. Luckily, Tweedledum and Tweedledee were there to help her out.

"The Walrus told me that one branch of this path would lead me to the Mad Hatter's house and that the other would take me to the den of the Jabberwock, a place I certainly don't want to go to. He said that you boys know the right path to take. He also warned me that one of you always tells the truth, and that the other one always lies. He also says that I can only ask of you one question." Alice then phrased her question in such a way that she was sure to get a correct answer regardless of which brother she asked. Can you figure out what question she put to the boys to get the right directions?

The World's Toughest "Math" Puzzle

$$1 - 2 = 3$$
$$4 \div 5 = 6$$
$$7 + 8 = 9$$

Alright class, pay attention! Your favorite substitute teacher, Ms. Priscilla Sunshine, is back with an extra credit math problem for you.

"Students, I've written an extremely interesting equation on the board for you to solve. Unfortunately, for you, I've placed the numbers one through nine in the wrong order. You must rearrange these numbers so that the four propositions pictured here are correct." (There are three horizontal equations and one vertical equation to set straight.)

The World's Toughest "Sea Horse" Puzzle

Six playful sea horses are lined up to play a little game. The first three have light-colored tails while the last three have dark-colored tails. What they want to do is to change positions in ten moves or less. Now a sea horse can move backwards or forward to the next adjacent position if it is empty and can swim over one or two other sea horses to get to a vacant position. When they're finished the first three positions should have three dark-tailed sea horses, the next three should have three light-tailed ones and the seventh position should be empty.

The problem looks easy but watch out, you might get hooked by it.

The World's Toughest "Tennis Ball" Puzzle

The other day Grand Slam Cooper, proprietor of the Hit & Miss Sport Shop, was checking out a new shipment of tennis balls when he noticed that each of the three crates was mislabelled. Being a puzzler of great renown he came up with a problem that has stumped everyone so far. It goes like this: Take one tennis ball out of anyone of the three crates without looking into the crate or into any of the other crates. With only the color of the one tennis ball to guide you, correctly label each of the crates.

See if you can net the answer in ten minutes. No overtime permitted.

The World's Toughest "Relation" Puzzle

> "Well, what do you think of it, Daphne? I commissioned William Farquar himself to paint it. Do you think it's a good likeness? It moves me to verse.
>   Sisters and brothers have I none,
>   But that man's father was my father's son."

The beaming gentleman above is certainly happy about his newly purchased work of art. However, the big question is, who is the person in the picture? What is the relationship between the art connoisseur here and the subject of his masterpiece?

The World's Toughest "Explorer" Puzzle

> Here, in the middle of this confounded desert, is the lost city of Ishtar. To reach it I will have to travel overland by foot from the coast. On a trek like this each man can only carry enough rations for five days and I calculate that the farthest we can travel in one day is 30 miles. The map that I obtained states that the city is 120 miles from my starting point. What I am trying to figure out is the fewest number of men, including myself, that I will need in our party so that I alone can reach the city, stay overnight, and then return to the coast without running out of supplies.

Can you discover the answer to this mystery?

The World's Toughest "Money" Puzzle

J. Wellington Moneybags, that Prince of Gamblers, is back with an interesting betting proposition for you. He claims that 1981 $100 bills are worth more today than 1980 $100 bills. Do you think that he's wrong? He's willing to wager you a $100 that he can prove it!

The World's Toughest "Watch" Puzzle

The little old watchmaker has dropped by to test your skills of precision and orderliness. He has arrayed nine examples of his noble profession, and his challenge is to arrange these timepieces into ten rows with three watches in each row. You'll get a big hand if you can sweep through this puzzle in less than 15 minutes.

The World's Toughest "Ice Cream Stick" Puzzle

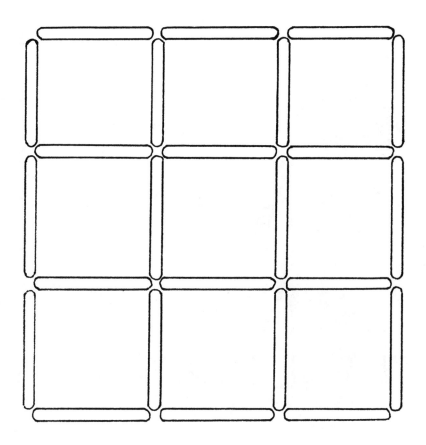

Here's an ice cream stick puzzle that will put you in a good humor if you can figure out the solution. We've arranged 24 sticks so that they form nine squares. Can you remove four of these sticks so that we are left with just five squares?

The World's Toughest "Contest" Puzzle

PUZZLE No. 77

Professor Doubtinger is seen here examining the winning entry to puzzle number 77 during last year's International Puzzle Contest. The Professor was making sure that the lines do not cross at any point in the solution. To check the Professor, draw the figure shown here using one continuous line. At no point can the line cross itself nor can you lift the pencil from the paper. You also cannot fold the paper at any point.

The World's Toughest "Target" Puzzle

Family fun at the turn of the century leads us to an interesting puzzle. Alexander and his sister Sybilla both put three of their rubber-tipped arrows in the same circles of the target and came up with a combined score of 96 points. Can you figure out which circles the arrows ended up in?

The World's Toughest "Counterfeit" Puzzle

Trusting Ned Armstrong, the owner of Ned's Wonderful World of Sports, made his first sale the other day to a somewhat suspicious looking gentleman. The customer purchased a package of golf balls for $12 and paid Ned with a $20 bill. Ned was all out of singles so he went next door to the bakery to change it; then he gave the customer his purchase and $8 in change. Ten minutes later the baker came in complaining that Ned had given him a counterfeit bill. Ned took back the bogus twenty and gave the baker a $20 bill from the register. Now, the big question in Ned's mind was just how much money had he lost on his first sale? Keep in mind that the markup on a package of golf balls is 100 percent.

The World's Toughest "Square" Puzzle

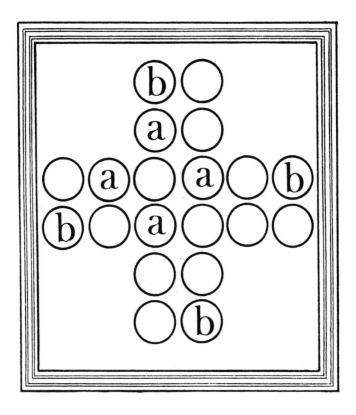

In the picture above we have twenty circles arranged in the form of a cross. How many perfect squares can you see in this cross when you consider any four circles as being the corners of a square? Look a the diagram and you will see what I mean. The four circles which contain the letter **a** form the corners of one square, and the four circles containing the letter **b** form another square. Altogether, you should be able to find 19 different squares in the drawing.

The World's Toughest "Orchard" Puzzle

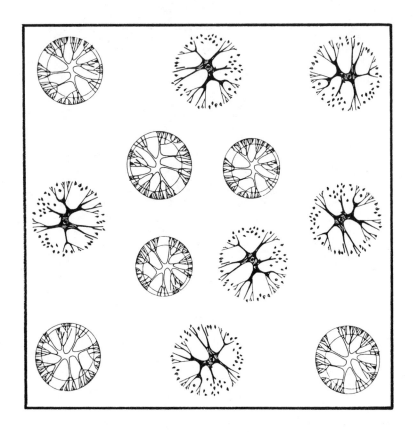

When that famous agriculturist, Farmer Brown, died, he specified that his holdings were to be equally divided among his four sons. He specifically stated that his orchard, which contained 12 prize fruit trees, was to be divided in such a manner that each portion was to be of the same size and shape and was to contain three of the trees. How did the sons fence off the orchard to comply with their father's wishes?

The World's Toughest "Cowboy" Puzzle

One night Sheriff Colt Remington came upon three cowboys sitting around a campfire. He suspected that one of them was the notorious cattle rustler, Tombstone Moe, while the other two were probably trail-hands looking for a job. From experience the sheriff knew that the two innocent cowboys would tell the truth if questioned and that Tombstone was sure to lie.

When the Sheriff asked the first man what he was doing, the cowboy muttered some answer and fainted dead away. The second man quickly spoke up. "He said that he's a cowpuncher and that's the truth! We're both cowpunchers!"

The third man now jumped up and pointed his finger at the second man shouting "That's not true. He's a darn liar!"

With that, Sheriff Remington grabbed one of the cowboys and slapped the cuffs on him saying, "I've heard enough, Tombstone. From now on you'll do your rustling behind the bars of the big state ranch at Abilene!" Which cowpoke did Sheriff Remington slap the darbees on?

The World's Toughest "Button" Puzzle

At the turn of the century no button was better than a Barton button, and here is one of their speedy delivery vans making its rounds. It was noted, even back then, that the pattern of buttons painted on the side of the van could be made into a puzzle. The ten buttons are in three rows with four buttons in each row (one horizontal row and two vertical rows). By moving only two of the buttons to new positions you can create four rows with four buttons in each row. See if you can fasten onto the solution within ten minutes.

The World's Toughest "Word" Puzzle

Happy Harrington, the Jolly Juggler, is bringing the house down with his word juggling puzzle. The problem is to use the ten letters printed on the balls to make first a one-letter word, then a two-letter word, and so on up to a ten-letter word. The spotlight is on and the curtain is going up! Start performing!

The World's Toughest "IQ" Puzzle

Here's a real IQ tester. Pictured above are six random (perhaps) patterns made up of circles, triangles and squares. The test is to determine what the next three patterns in the series will be. On your mark, get set, start drawing!

The World's Toughest "Placement" Puzzle

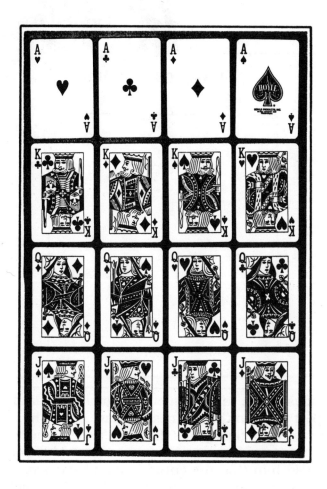

This wonderful problem is well over 100 years old. You are required to take the 16 cards shown above and place them in four rows of four cards each. This must be done in such a way that no two cards of the same value, or of the same suit, are in any horizontal, vertical or diagonal row of four cards.

The World's Toughest "Robbery Plans" Puzzle

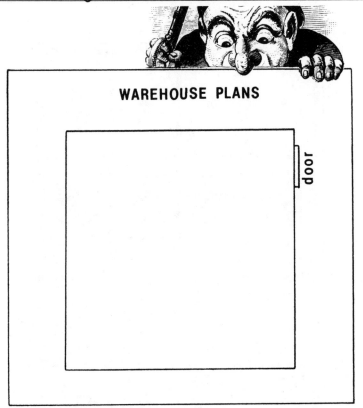

WAREHOUSE PLANS

door

Warehouse Willy, that infamous safecracker, was also the cheapest crook in the business. To save money he bought a cut-rate set of floor plans that didn't show where any of the rooms were in a warehouse he intended to rob. The seller told him that the entire building was square and that the main room had a door to the outside. Inside, the warehouse floor plan is divided into six square rooms. Four of the smaller rooms have doors opening into the main room. The fifth small room contained the safe. The seller told Willie that all he had to do to complete the floor plan was to draw four straight lines across the square shown in the above plan. Where do the lines go?

The World's Toughest "Distance" Puzzle

Merlin, the great All-Knowing Wizard of King Arthur's Court, brings out the next mystery: Take four English pennies and arrange them in such a way that every coin is equidistant from every other coin. (If you don't happen to have any English pennies handy, quarters or half-dollars will do just as well.)

The World's Toughest "Toothpick" Puzzle

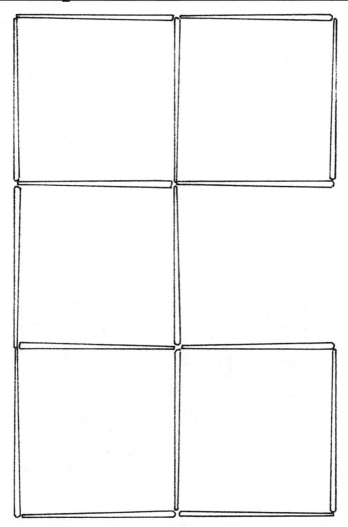

Here's an interesting little puzzle that should keep you busy for a few minutes . . . or more. Above are six squares constructed from sixteen toothpicks. Your job is to move three of these toothpicks to new positions so that we now have four equal squares.

The World's Toughest "Chess" Puzzle

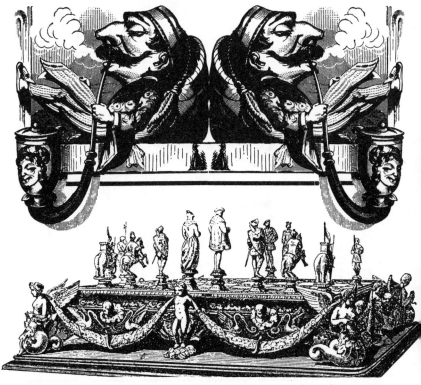

The Puff Brothers are not speaking to each other since Bertram won a chess bet from Augustus. Up until last Friday Bertram had never beaten Augustus at chess. Here's how he challenged his brother on that fateful day:

"Augustus, I'll bet you a tin of your favorite tobacco that I can simultaneously play two chess games with you and either win one of the games or draw both of them. The only stipulations I make are that we alternate our moves on two separate chessboards and that on one board I play black while on the other board I play white. Finally, to show you how confident I am, I will give you the honor of going first. Are you game for a game?"

How did Bertram puff his way to victory?

The World's Toughest "Clown" Puzzle

T	W	L	H	A	O	U	L
E							G
S							A
H							H
A							U
A							S
T	L	S	S	E	H	B	G

Chuckles the Clown is here to entertain you. What he doesn't know about making people laugh isn't worth knowing. With this in mind he has selected a famous quotation and arranged it into this puzzle. See if you can find the quotation in the above frame of letters. Starting at any letter, go around the frame twice reading every other letter as you go. Don't take a pratfall on this one!

The World's Toughest "Farmer" Puzzle

Squire Murdock was a gentleman farmer of some renown around these parts. He was also something of an eccentric. Here he's studying the plans for a new enclosure for his nine prized heifers. He told his men that they had to build four fenced-in enclosures to hold the cows, but each enclosure must contain an uneven number of cows. Can you figure out how the men solved this cantankerous problem?

The World's Toughest "Cake" Puzzle

To celebrate the founding of the Plymouth Colony pilgrim Thomas Tinker devised the following puzzle: The prize winning cake at the annual Plymouth Bakeoff must be cut into eight equal-sized pieces with just 3 cuts of Governor Bradford's broadsword. Alright pilgrim, let's see what progress you can make with this puzzle.

The World's Toughest "Scholars" Puzzle

Professor, I think you'll find that this is a devilishly hard word puzzle to solve. Give me a word that contains five consonants in a row.

"That is a tough one, professor, but you'll have to line up to get the answer to my latest problem, namely, what word contains five vowels in a row?"

The World's Toughest "Prediction" Puzzle

CATEGORIES

① A, M...

② B,C,D,E,K,

③ F,G,J,L...

④ H,I...

Alright, Madam Wanda, solve this one if you can. On this paper are the first thirteen letters of the alphabet divided into four categories. Can you, in all your infinite wisdom, predict which of the four categories each of the remaining thirteen letters should be placed in?

The World's Toughest "Answerless" Puzzle

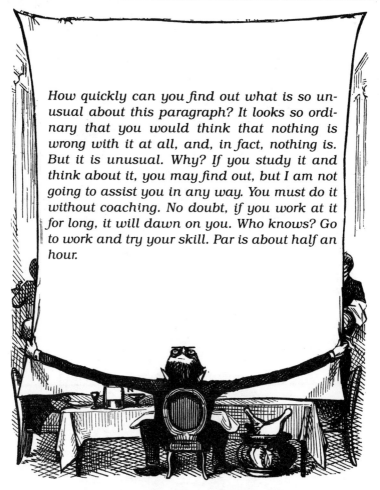

How quickly can you find out what is so unusual about this paragraph? It looks so ordinary that you would think that nothing is wrong with it at all, and, in fact, nothing is. But it is unusual. Why? If you study it and think about it, you may find out, but I am not going to assist you in any way. You must do it without coaching. No doubt, if you work at it for long, it will dawn on you. Who knows? Go to work and try your skill. Par is about half an hour.

Quimby Sureye, the editor of a local puzzle magazine, is at his wit's end. The above puzzle was submitted without an answer, and Quimby's been trying to solve it for over a week. Day and night, wherever he goes, Quimby's been studying it without success. Can you solve this perplexing problem and bring tranquility back into Quimby's life?

The World's Toughest "Number" Puzzle

Ruppert, the famous talking rhino, has come up with a new puzzle that should keep you busy for quite a while. Arrange the four numbers 2, 3, 4, and 5, along with a plus sign and an equal sign, into a valid mathematical equation.

The World's Toughest "River" Puzzle

Ezra Walton, skipper of the Speedy Water Taxi Service, was transporting Herbie Bakewell up river to his new business location. As soon as the boat left the dock Herbie fell asleep. After the boat had traveled one mile Herbie's hat blew off into the water and started floating back downstream. The boat continued upstream for five more minutes before Herbie woke up and discovered that his hat was missing. Herbie then made Ezra turn around and head back downstream. They finally caught up with the hat just as it reached their original starting point. The sailing speed of Ezra's boat was constant whether going upstream or downstream. With these facts to work with can you figure out how fast the river was flowing?

The World's Toughest "Hidden Sentence" Puzzle

PUZZLE #1

$\dfrac{STAND}{I}$ $\dfrac{TAKE}{YOU}$ $\dfrac{MINE}{2}$ $\dfrac{STANDING.}{MY}$

PUZZLE #2

10   20   04   18   0

Tommy and Rusty are shown here rushing two new puzzles over to the editor of the *World Puzzle Gazette* newspaper. Each of the puzzles is really a mathematical expression that encodes a grammatically complete English sentence. Can you break the codes and tell what message is to be found on each sign?

The World's Toughest "Jumping" Puzzle

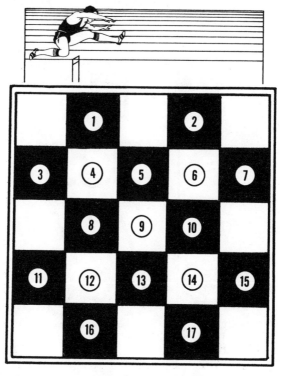

Let's see if you can hurdle to victory on this.   Lay out a small checkerboard as shown above and place a checker on every square that has a number in it. The problem is, starting with the checker in square 9, remove all of the checkers from the board, save one, and have this last checker end up where you started in square 9. You can jump one checker over another checker in any direction, sideways, up and down, or diagonally. Whenever you jump over a checker you must remove it from the board. However, as in checkers, the square beyond the checker you are jumping over must be empty. A continuous series of jumps, using one checker, will count as one move. Solve the puzzle in just four moves.

The World's Toughest "Elimination" Puzzle

$$111$$
$$333$$
$$777$$
$$\underline{999}$$

Maude Wheeler turned up at the annual Costume and Puzzle Ball dressed as a pirate and proceeded to keelhaul everyone in sight with her puzzle entry. The problem went as follows: Remove five of the twelve numbers in the addition problem pictured above so that the remaining numbers will add up to 1111. (Maude preferred the term "Gut 'em out!" but simply crossing them out will also suffice.) If you don't want to walk the plank, solve it in under thirty minutes.

The World's Toughest "Rearranging Bee" Puzzle

KLASAA
LHATDAIN
INDIRTDA

ACGIUNAAR
RUSLAITAA
RISACFOAUHT

ADEKMRN
GRBAAILU
HPEITIAO

DAUROHNS
HFNNAASTGAI
SHININECLTEET

Get set for a "rearranging bee" puzzler! Listed around the globe above are the names of eleven different countries and one of the United States of America. For our test we've scrambled the letters in each name. It's up to you to rearrange them correctly. Ten out of twelve will confirm that you are indeed a seasoned traveller.

The World's Toughest "Circle" Puzzle

Professor Melbourne is contemplating an ancient puzzle brought to class by one of his students. The problem: Take the numbers 1 through 12 and place them in the twelve circles depicted in the diagram. The catch is that the sum of the numbers in the outer circle must be twice as large as the sum of the numbers in the inner circle; and the four inner numbers must be in consecutive order.

The World's Toughest "Skating" Puzzle

Willard Wonderwheels was the winner of the 1889 Roller Puzzle Ball. He is shown here wearing his first prize trophy. Willard's winning feat, which has not been surpassed to this day, is also pictured above. While skating backwards he was able to duplicate the design pictured in fewer continuous strokes than anyone else at the ball that night. With a pencil and paper, figure out how many strokes it took Willard to win the coveted prize without lifting the pencil from the paper. Every time the pencil changes direction it is a new stroke. Drawing the outer circle is considered one stroke, and you will have to draw over the same line more than once.

The World's Toughest "Boarding House" Puzzle

Mr. Williams, Mr. Barnet and Mr. Edwards all live in Ma Boscombs boarding house. One is a baker, one a taxi driver and one a fireman. Which is which is for you to figure out. Here are five clues to help:

1. Mr. Williams and Mr. Barnet play chess every night.
2. Mr. Barnet and Mr. Edwards go to baseball games together.
3. The taxi driver collects coins, the fireman lead soldiers, and the baker stamps.
4. The taxi driver has never seen a ball game.
5. Mr. Edwards has never heard of approvals.

The World's Toughest "Plywood" Puzzle

Hiram Ballpeene, our local handyman, was hired by Ma Boscomb to replace a section of floor in her attic. He had to cover an opening that was 2-feet wide and 12-feet long. In his truck Hiram had a sheet of plywood that was 3-feet wide and 8-feet long. Being a master carpenter Hiram was able to cut this board into two pieces which covered the hole perfectly. How did he do it?

The World's Toughest "Utility" Puzzle

WATER

GAS

ELECTRICITY

Back when they built the above three houses they had some pretty stiff building codes. When it came to connecting the water, gas and underground electric lines to each house the builder was told that none of the lines could cross under, through or over any of the other lines. It took him over a week to figure out how he could do it and stay within the letter of the law. How did he dig himself out of this municipal predicament?

The World's Toughest "Paradox" Puzzle

THE PLAYERS WHO ALL WON

As an improvement upon the accepted notion that winners can only gain as much as the losers lose, Sam Loyd* took occasion to call attention to a more profitable style of play. Pay attention to the following narration:

"Four jolly men sat down to play,
And played all night till break of day;
They played for gold and not for fun,
With separate scores for every one,
Yet, when they came to square accounts,
They all had made quite fair amounts!
Can you the paradox explain?
If no one lost, how could all gain?"

*The above problem is by America's greatest creator of puzzles, Sam Loyd.

The World's Toughest "Clock" Puzzle

Pictured here is a product of the Olde Reliable Clock Company. *Unreliable* would be a more appropriate name for them since there are several errors in the clock's manufacture. Your problem is to correctly locate each and every defect in this forgettable timepiece. If you miss one of the errors you will fail our test. You have 60 seconds to arrive at a correct count.

The World's Toughest "Speed" Puzzle

Mad Man Moriarty, an early motoring madcap, is shown here negotiating the hazardous road down from atop of Old Baldy Mountain. When all's well with his vintage vehicle Moriarty can leave his home in Hooterville, climb up one side of Old Baldy at a steady 10 miles per hour and descend, on the other side, at an equally steady 20 miles an hour. If Moriarty turned around and came right back to Hooterville what would his average speed for the round-trip be?

The World's Toughest "Allowance" Puzzle

All right, son, I've got a puzzle for you, and if you can solve it, I'll double your allowance for the week. I'm placing a quarter and a dime in the middle of the table, and I'll bet that you can't put the dime under the quarter without touching the quarter with anything including your fingers. Do you think that you can solve this mystery?

That's easy, Dad!
Let's do this every week!

The World's Toughest "Transpositional" Puzzle

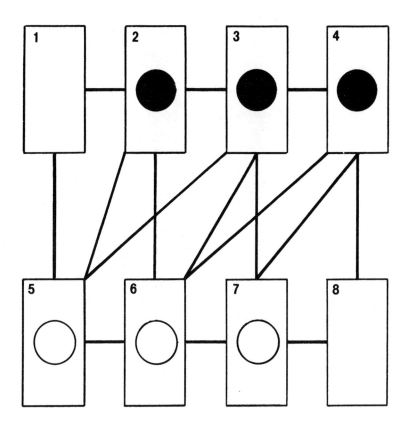

Here's one of those transpositional puzzles that we all love (?) so well. First place three pennies on the black spots in boxes 2, 3, and 4; then place three dimes on the white spots in boxes 5, 6, and 7. Now make them change places in just seven moves, moving the coins from one box to another along the heavy lines that connect them and only moving a coin to an empty box.

The World's Toughest "Brick Wall" Puzzle

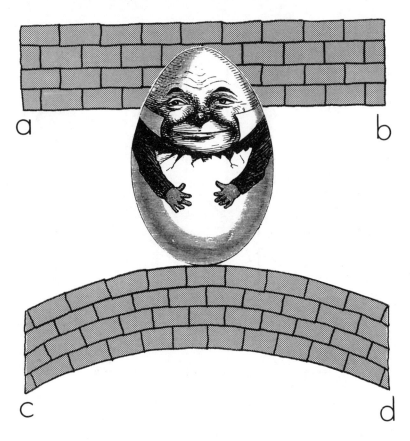

The other day Humpty Dumpty called in a mason and asked him to build two brick walls in his garden. Both walls were to be the same height and distance. (The length of **ab** is equal to **cd**). The mason said that he would have to charge more for wall **cd** since it stood on a hill and would need more materials to construct.

"Nonsense," said Mr. Dumpty, "it should cost less since you will need fewer bricks and mortar to build it!"

Who do you think is right? Is this a case for Trevor Torts, practising attorney?

The World's Toughest "Arranging" Puzzle

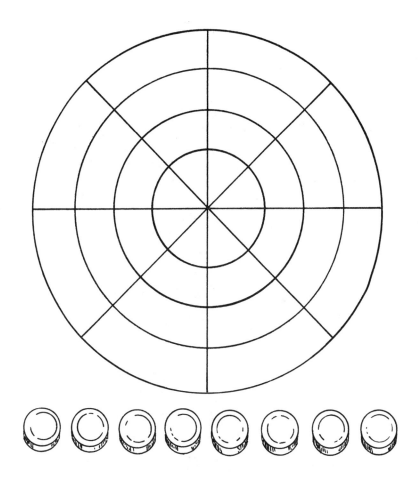

Here's an interesting problem in arranging. Make a larger copy of the drawing and use eight checkers as counters. Now place the checkers on the various lines of the drawing so that there are two checkers on every circle and two checkers on every one of the four straight lines.

The World's Toughest "Summing" Puzzle

To solve this puzzle, come up with an unconventional solution to what, at first glance, will seem to be an impossible problem. Take all the numbers 1 through 9 and place them in two columns so that the sum of each column will be the same.

The World's Toughest "Hidden Words" Puzzle

Ah! _If I_ get my good ship home
  I'll find a tempting rural spot,
Where mayhap pleasant flowers will bloom,
  And there I'll shape a charming cot.
Where bees sip nectar in each flower,
  And Philomel on hawthorn rests,
I'll shape a rustic, sun-kissed bower—
  A bower meet for angel guest.
Then she who lives and loves with me,
  Sing our days of calm repose,
Sole monarch of the flowers will be—
  For Myra is indeed a rose.

In this poem are twelve "hidden" words, each word being the name of a fruit. There is one word in each of the twelve lines of the poem, usually beginning in one word and finishing up in the next word. As an example, the word in the first sentence is _fig_. It's underlined to make it clearer.

The World's Toughest "Trolley" Puzzle

Amos Fastchange, a conductor on the old Metropolitan Trolley Line, used to entertain his passengers with puzzles during their travels. His favorite one went something like this.

"In my hand I'm holding the largest sum of money, in good ol' American coins, that you can have at one time without being able to give change for a dollar, a half-dollar, a quarter, a dime or a nickel. None of these coins is a silver dollar. Let's see if you can calculate this amount before we get to the next stop."

The World's Toughest "What Am I" Puzzle

> *Twice ten are six of us,*
> *Six are but three of us,*
> *Nine are but four of us;*
>   *What can we possibly be?*
> *Would you know more of us,*
> *Twelve are but six of us,*
>   *Five are but four, do you see?*

The famous Three Bavarian Bafflers have put their favorite puzzle to song. Can you discern what the mysterious items referred to in this platinum record could possibly be?

The World's Toughest "Easter Egg" Puzzle

Wow! There's a swell toy inside this Easter Egg!

Jimmy, the Honest Newsboy, asked the store owner if he could buy just the toy and not the egg. The pastry maker told him that the price of the stuffed egg was $4.50 and that the cost of the egg alone was $4 more than the cost of the toy inside. How much did Jimmy have to pay for the toy?

The World's Toughest "Swapping" Puzzle

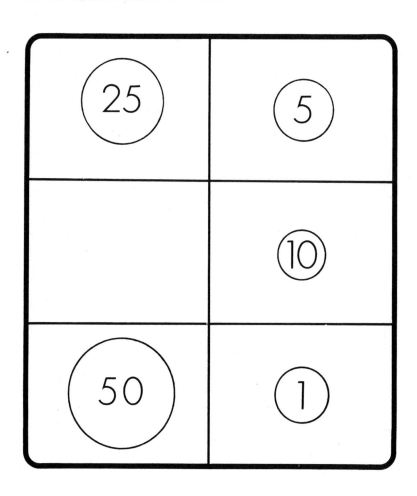

Lay out a puzzle board similar to the six-paneled one pictured and place a half-dollar, a quarter, a dime, a nickel and a penny in the partitions indicated. By sliding the coins one at a time into a vacant space, make the half-dollar and the penny change places, shifting only in a horizontal or a vertical direction.

The World's Toughest "Knight" Puzzle

In the drawing is a segment from a chessboard with two white knights in squares 1 and 3 and two black knights in squares 7 and 9. The problem, using only knight's moves, is to exchange the positions of the black and white pieces in seven moves.

ANSWERS

"Surveyor" puzzle (page 6): Draw a straight line from point **A** to point **D**. Point **D** is the midpoint of line **C-E**. This gives us the triangle **A-B-D**, which is half of the rectangle made up of side **AB** and side **BD**.

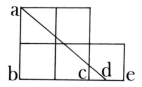

"Mental" Puzzle (page 7): It's really easy to be a mental wizard. Here's how: The sum of the four numbers is 23. All you have to do is subtract this sum from the next highest multiple of 9. In this case that would be 27. So, subtracting 23 from 27 gives us 4, the number that was crossed out. It works every time.

"Poem" puzzle (page 8): Alas, the impossible is still impossible. In the confusion of the poem, at no time did it mention placing *the tenth man* in a room. Rather, it states that the landlord went back to the first room, where he had lodged man *one* and man *two*, and referred to one of them as *the tenth man*. I guess that the real tenth man ended up sleeping in the barn.

"Penguin" puzzle (page 9):

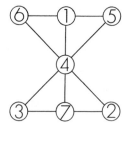

"Match" puzzle (page 10):

78

"Coin" puzzle (page 11): Place a finger on the middle coin in the top row and slide the coin upwards and to the left. Keep sliding the coin around and down the left column of coins. Finally, slide it around the bottom and bring it into position beneath the middle coin in the bottom row. Now push the entire middle column of coins upward until you once again have four rows of 3 coins each. Each row will now have only all heads or all tails in it. During the entire operation you only touched one coin. Amazing!

"Paper" puzzle (page 12): Take a stiff sheet of white paper and make three cuts in it as shown in the drawing. Each cut stops in the middle of the sheet. Now fold flap **A**, along the middle line, up to edge **BB**. Finally, take side **C** and rotate it 180°. Place the paper down onto the table and you will find that you have created the famous "Paper Impossibility." It is most effective when glued down on top of a dark sheet of red or blue paper. The flap, of course, should be left unglued.

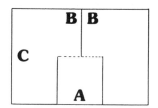
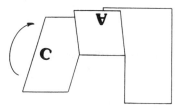

"Portrait" puzzle (page 13):

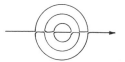

"Change" puzzle (page 14): This is a "gotcha" type of puzzle. The coin that "is not a nickel" is, of course, a half-dollar. The other coin is a nickel. How else?

"Progression" puzzle (page 15): You have no bats in your belfry if you solved this one. The numbers represent the chimes of a clock that strikes once on the half hour. The next four notes (or numbers) are, 1, 4, 1 and 5.

"Archaeology" puzzle (page 16): The answer to this one is as old as puzzling itself . . . it's man. As a baby he crawls on all fours, in his prime he walks on two legs, and at twilight he walks with the aid of a cane.

"Bell Ringer's" puzzle (page 17): It will take the brothers exactly 56¼ seconds to toll ten o'clock. Here's how it works: Between striking one and five there are four intervals. Therefore dividing four into the total time of 25 seconds we get 6¼ seconds per interval. Now, between striking one and ten there are nine intervals. So, if we multiply nine times 6¼ seconds we get a total of 56¼ seconds, the time it takes to strike ten o'clock.

"Talisman" puzzle (page 18):

"Checker" puzzle (page 19): White to move and win as follows: 15 to 10, 24 to 6, 7 to 2, 12 to 19, and 2 to 27.

"Triangle" puzzle (page 20): By removing the four bars indicated in the drawing with dotted lines you will be left with four triangles of equal size.

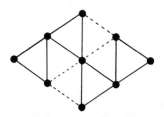

"Stocking" puzzle (page 21): The total number of stockings that Rojer had to take from the bottom drawer was three. If the first two stockings matched he had no problem. If not, the third stocking would match one of the first two stockings. Either way Rodger would be sure to arrive at his duel in sartorially splendor as usual.

"Measuring" puzzle (page 22): Here's what Pester Pew should have done;

1) Fill up the three-gallon jug; then pour the three gallons into the five-gallon cask.

2) Refill the three-gallon jug and once again pour it's contents into the five-gallon cask until the cask is full.

3) The three-gallon jug now contains one gallon. Empty the five-gallon cask back into the rum vat; then pour the one gallon from the three-gallon jug into it.

4) Finally, fill the three-gallon jug up again; then pour its contents into the five-gallon cask. The cask will now have the desired four gallons that Billy Bones came ashore to purchase.

"Alice" puzzle (page 23): Alice asked, "If I had asked you yesterday, 'Which is the path that will lead me to the house of the Mad Hatter?' what would your answer have been?"

To such a question the truthful brother would again give the correct answer. The untruthfull brother, however, would have to tell a lie as to what he would have answered the day before which, at that time, would also have been a lie. So his offsetting lie would also have been the correct path to take. Well done, Alice!

"Math" puzzle (page 24):

$$9 - 5 = 4$$
$$\times$$
$$6 \div 3 = 2$$
$$=$$
$$1 + 7 = 8$$

"Sea Horse" puzzle (page 25): The winning moves go like this: Move 2 to 1; 5 to 2; 3 to 5; 6 to 3; 7 to 6; 4 to 7; 1 to 4; 3 to 1; 6 to 3; 7 to 6. The sea horses have now changed position and space 7 is empty.

"Tennis Ball" puzzle (page 26): The one thing to keep in mind is that every box is mislabeled. Start by taking a tennis ball from the box labeled "White & Yellow Tennis Balls." Let's say that the color of the ball is yellow. Take the

"Yellow Tennis Balls" label and put it on the box you just removed the ball from, then remove the "White & Yellow Tennis Balls" label and put it on one of the remaining two boxes. But which one? If you put it on the box that the "Yellow Tennis Balls" label came from then that would mean that the label on the box marked "White Tennis Balls" couldn't be changed and that would be incorrect since *every* box is known to be mislabeled. So, move the "White Tennis Balls" label to the unlabeled box and put the "White & Yellow Tennis Balls" label on the box that was labeled "White Tennis Balls." If the ball removed from the first box had been white then the same logic would prevail in moving the labels around. Tennis anyone?

"Relation" puzzle (page 27): The person pictured in the portrait is the son of the gentleman who bought the painting.

"Explorer" puzzle (page 28): Our intrepid explorer will need three other men in his party to accomplish his mission. Here's how the marching orders will go:

4 men × 5 day's rations = 20 day's rations.

First day—Four day's rations are used up. One man goes back using one day's ration for the return trip.

Second day—Remaining three men use up three day's rations. One man goes back using two day's rations for the return trip.

Third day—Remaining two men use up two day's rations. One man goes back using three day's rations for the return trip.

Fourth day—Remaining man uses up one day's rations. He reaches city and stays the night. The next day he returns to coast using up four day's rations.

"Money" puzzle (page 29): J. Wellington is right of course. 1981 $100 bills are worth $198,100, while 1980 $100 bills are only worth $198,000. Did he catch you on that one?

"Watch" puzzle (page 30):

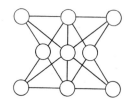

"Ice Cream Stick" puzzle (page 31):

"Contest" puzzle (page 32):

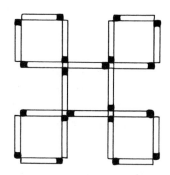

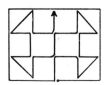

"Target" puzzle (page 33): Alexander and Sybilla scored as follows; two arrows in the 25 circle, two arrows in the 20 circle, and two arrows in the 3 circle.

"Counterfeit" puzzle (page 34): Ned is out exactly $14. The golf balls cost Ned $6 and he gave $8 in change to the shy gentleman. Live and learn, Ned!

"Square" puzzle (page 35): There are 19 different squares indicated in the drawing below. There are four **a** type squares, two **b** type squares, nine **c** type squares, and four **d** type squares.

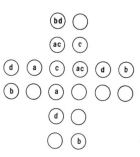

"Orchard" puzzle (page 36):

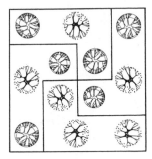

"Cowboy" puzzle (page 37): The third cowpoke was the one that the sheriff took into custody. He figured that the statement of the second cowboy had to be true; otherwise the first *and* second cowboys were liars and they were both rustlers. This the sheriff knew couldn't be true since he was sure that there was only one rustler at large in his territory.

"Button" puzzle (page 38): The drawing shows which two buttons to reposition.

"Word" puzzle (page 39): The following ten words nicely satisfy Happy Harrington's bouncing problem; I, do, met, shot, timed, desist, methods, moistest, Methodist, Methodists.

"IQ" puzzle (page 40): Each pattern represents a number. In the first pattern there are three circles which gives us the number 3. The second pattern has one triangle, giving us the number 1. The rest of the patterns yield up the numbers 4, 1, 5, 9 or, the value of Pi to five places. The next three patterns would therefore be two nested circles, six nested triangles and five nested squares. (The shapes of the patterns go in order: circle, triangle and square.)

"Placement" puzzle (page 41): The winning arrangement of cards is as follows;

JD	QC	KH	AS
KS	AH	JC	QD
AC	KD	QS	JH
QH	JS	AD	KC

"Robbery Plans" puzzle (page 42):

"Distance" puzzle (page 43): Place three of the coins in a triangle so that each coin is touching the other two coins. Now, place the fourth coin in the center, on top of the other three coins. Since every coin is now touching every other coin, the coins are all equidistant from each other.

"Toothpick" puzzle (page 44):

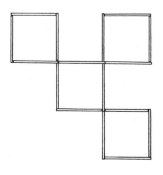

"Chess" puzzle (page 45): Here's how Bertram did it. Augustus opened with a white move on board one. Bertram promptly made the same opening move with white on board two. Augustus made his answering black move on board two. Bertram made this same answering move with black on board one. Back and forth they went with Bertram always using Augustus' moves on one board as his moves on the other board. Finally Augustus realized that he was playing himself and that if he won one of the games he would also lose the other game, or, he could draw both games. In no case could he hope to win both of the games. In disgust he gave up and swore that he'd never play chess with his brother again.

"Clown" puzzle (page 46): Starting with the "H" on the left side of Chuckle's picture, read around the frame clockwise. The rather apt quotation is, "He who laughs last laughs best!"

"Farmer" puzzle (page 47): The men built three enclosures and placed three heifers in each of them; then they built a fourth enclosure around the first three. In that way all of the enclosures came to hold an odd number of heifers.

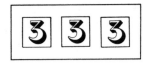

"Cake" puzzle (page 48): Well, pilgrim, here's how it's done: First, one swift cut horizontally through the middle of the cake with Bradford's broadsword yields us two large pieces. Thomas follows up with two vertical cuts at right angles to one another to finish off the puzzle. The result is eight equal pieces of delicious Plymouth cake.

"Scholars" puzzles (page 49): The first scholar gives us a clue when he mentions that the answer is "devilishly" hard to solve. The word is "witchcraft." The second scholar also dropped a clue when he said that you will have to "line up" to get the answer. His word was "queueing."

"Prediction" puzzle (page 50): I'm sorry to report that Madam Wanda's crystal ball was clouded and she failed to divine the correct answer. The result she was looking for goes like this: Category one has letters **AMTUVWY**. All of these letters have symmetry about their vertical axis. Category two has letters **BCDEK**. They have symmetry about their horizontal axis. Category three has letters **FGJLNP-QRSZ**. They have no symmetry about any axis. Finally, category four has letters **HIOX**. They have symmetry about both their vertical and horizontal axis.

"Answerless" puzzle (page 51): Shame on Quimby, and shame on you if you missed this one. The letter "e," the most used of all the letters, is missing from the text of the puzzle that Quimby is editing.

"Number" puzzle (page 52): Ruppert's solution goes like this: $3^2 = 4 + 5$. This of course gives us $9 = 9$, a valid equation.

"River" puzzle (page 53): Any method of solution will show that the speed of the boat is irrelevant to the solution. The best solution is arrived at when one looks at the problem from Herbie's vantage point: To Herbie the hat is just sitting there in the water. First he sails away from it for five minutes, then he turns around and sails back for five minutes and picks it up. During that time the hat has traveled downstream one mile on the river current. It took the hat 10 minutes to travel that mile so we can calculate from that that the river was flowing at a rate of 6 miles per hour.

"Hidden Sentence puzzles (page 54): The coded sentence in the first puzzle is: "I understand you undertake to undermine my understanding."

The coded second sentence in the second puzzle is: "One ought to owe nothing, for one ate nothing."

"Jumping puzzle (page 55): The answer goes like this: For your first move jump 9 over 13, 14, 6, 4, 3, 1, 2, 7, 15, 17, 16, 11. Remove all pieces jumped. The next move is 12 over 8. The third play is 10 over 5 and 12. The final jump is 9 over 10 landing checker 9 back where it started.

"Elimination" puzzle (page 56): Here's one solution to Maudie's problem. For the sake of alignment consider the numbers that have been removed by zeroes.

$$
\begin{array}{r}
111 \\
3 \\
7 \\
\underline{99} \\
1111
\end{array}
$$

"Rearranging Bee" puzzle (page 57): Our global answers are as follows:

KLASAA = ALASKA
LHATDAIN = THAILAND
INDIRTDA = TRINIDAD
ACGIUNAAR = NICARAGUA
RUSLAITAA = AUSTRALIA
RISACFOAUHT = SOUTH AFRICA
ADEKMRN = DENMARK
GRBAAILU = BULGARIA
HPEITIAO = ETHIOPIA
DAUROHNS = HONDURAS
SHININECLTEET = LIECHTENSTEIN
HFNNAASTGAI = AFGHANISTAN

"Circle" puzzle (page 58): The numbers in the inner circle are 5, 6, 7 and 8 which give us a total of 26. The numbers in the outer circle are 1, 2, 3, 4, 9, 10, 11 and 12 which give us a total of 52. This is exactly twice the total of the numbers in the inner circle. Puzzle solved!

"Skating" puzzle (page 59): The puzzle can be solved using twelve strokes. In the figure below start at point **A** and follow the lines around to point **B**. The two curved lines are drawn one above the other.

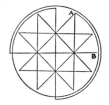

"Boarding House" puzzle (page 60): Since the taxi driver has never seen a ball game he must be Mr. Williams. Also, Mr. Edwards has never heard of approvals so he can't be a stamp collector. Therefore, the three occupations are: Mr. Williams is a taxi driver; Mr. Edwards is a fireman, and Mr. Barnet is a baker.

"Plywood" puzzle (page 61): Cut the board as indicated in Fig. 1 and shift the two pieces around as shown in Fig. 2. Hiram could now cover the hole perfectly.

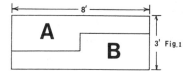

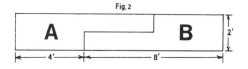

"Utility" puzzle (page 62): To solve this one the builder was forced to run one of the lines, from the water works, underneath house number 1 to house number 3. After that, all the rest was easy.

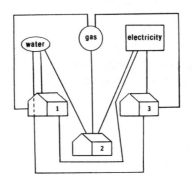

"Paradox" puzzle (page 63): The answer, according to Sam Loyd, was simple; the four men were all fiddlers in a German band and were each paid $5 at the end of the night for their endeavors (wages circa 1900). The puzzle does not say that they were gambling at cards although that is the usual assumption of the reader.

"The Clock" puzzle (page 64): The Olde Reliable Clock has an unlucky seven errors:

1) The hour hand is between hours when the minute hand is at 12.

2) Only four minutes are indicated between 3 and 4.

3) The alarm setting hand is not centered correctly.

4) The 6 should be a 7.

5) The 8 is at an angle.

6) There's an "X" instead of a 10 at ten o'clock.

7) The alarm clapper-hammer is outside of the bell.

"Speed" puzzle (page 65): The answer is arrived at by dividing the total distance Moriarty travelled by the total time of the journey. Let's say that the road on each side of Old Baldy Mountain was twenty miles long from base to top. It would take Moriarty two hours to reach the top and one hour to reach the bottom. Since the return trip would also take three hours the total time for the trip is six hours. During that time he would have travelled a distance of eighty miles. The average speed then is 80 miles in 6 hours, which comes to 13⅓ miles per hour.

"Allowance" puzzle (page 66): Quick as a flash Junior took the dime and placed it on the floor under the table. "There, Dad, I placed the dime under the quarter without touching it! As for my allowance, I'll take it in singles please."

"Transpositional" puzzle (page 67): The winning moves are: 2 to 1, 6 to 2, 4 to 6, 7 to 4, 3 to 7, 5 to 3 and 1 to 5.

"Brick Wall" puzzle (page 68): Wall **ab** is the same length as wall **bc**. If wall **bc** was sliced along the dotted line **1** and the upper section moved down to dotted line **2** we would have a brick wall of the same dimensions as wall **ab**. This clearly proves that both walls contain the same amount of material and thus should cost the same to build. Both Mr. Dumpty and the mason were wrong.

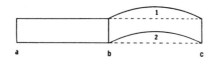

"Arranging" puzzle (page 69):

"Summing" puzzle (page 70): The columns may be slightly out of line but they answer the problem nicely.

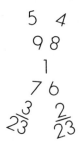

"Hidden Words" puzzle (page 71): The following words will be found within the poem:
Ah! If I get my good ship home (fig)
   I'll find a tempting rural spot, (date)
Where mayhap pleasant flowers will bloom, (apple)
   And there I'll shape a charming cot. (peach)
Where bees sip nectar in each flower, (nectarine)
   And Philomel on hawthorn rests, (melon)
I'll shape a rustic, sun-kissed bower—(pear)
   A bower meet for angel guests. (orange)
Then she who lives and loves with me, (olive)
   Sing our days of calm repose, (gourd)
Sole monarch of the flowers will be—(lemon)
   For Myra is indeed a rose." (raisin)

"Trolley" puzzle (page 72): The amount of change that Amos was holding came to $1.19. This amount was made up of a half dollar, a quarter, four dimes, and four pennies.

"What Am I" puzzle (page 73): The items in question are letters. In the first line twice ten is twenty, a word made up of six letters. In the word six there are three and in the word nine there are four, and so on with the remaining lines.

"Easter Egg" puzzle (page 74): The toy costs 25¢ and the egg costs $4.25, which is $4 more than the cost of the toy.

"Swapping" puzzle (page 75): First, slide all of the coins clockwise until the half-dollar is in the upper left-hand corner (Fig. A). Next, slide only the penny, nickel and the dime around clockwise until the penny is in the lower right-hand corner. Use only the bottom four squares for this shifting (Fig. B). Now slide the dime, the half-dollar and the quarter around clockwise, using only the upper four squares, until the coins are in the position shown in Fig. C. Your last move is to slide all of the coins clockwise one position and you will have the problem solved.

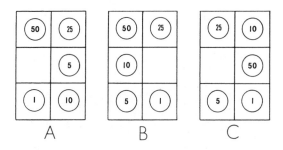

"Knight" puzzle (page 76): Moving the day knight moves, this combination gets the job done: 1–6, 3–8–1, 9–4–3–8, 7–2–9–4–3, 6–7–2–9, 1–6–7, 8–1

About the Author

Charles Barry Townsend has been writing books and editing magazines on puzzles, games and magic for over 15 years. He is the author of nine books including *The World's Best Puzzles* and *The World's Most Challenging Puzzles*, and for three years his monthly column "Puzzles and Problems" has graced the pages of *Creative Computing* and *Sync* magazines. He currently lives in Hilton Head Island, S.C., where he is presently publishing a quarterly puzzle magazine entitled *The Island Puzzler*. For information concerning this lively new addition to the world of puzzling and gaming literature please write to:

The Island Puzzler Magazine
P.O. Box 6591
Hilton Head, South Carolina 29938

Mr. and Mrs. Puzzler take a day off in the sun

INDEX